Wakefield Press

Tales from the Labyrinth

Peter Lloyd was born in the English Midlands and emigrated to Australia in the late 1970s. Most of his working life has been dedicated to providing housing for the under-privileged. He lives in the Adelaide Hills and is married with two children. Peter has had work published in Australia, Canada, the United States, the United Kingdom and France.

… in Peter Lloyd's hands, outrage at our blasted and despoiled world is turned into lightning-shafts of poetry.
J.M. Coetzee

The palette of a lifetime: powerful, achingly mature and enormously entertaining.
Stephen Lawrence, *Wet Ink*

A master craftsman. I can't remember the last time I encountered such seamless technical ability in an Australian poet.
Justin Lowe, *Thylazine*

Head and shoulders above the rest.
Glen Murdoch

By the same author

Black Swans (1997)

Collage (2002)

A Fingerpost for Rembrandt (2004)

Tales from the Labyrinth

Peter Lloyd

Wakefield Press

Wakefield Press
1 The Parade West
Kent Town
South Australia 5067
www.wakefieldpress.com.au

First published 2008

Typeset by Michael Deves, Lythrum Press, Adelaide
Printed and bound by Hyde Park Press

ISBN 978 1 86254 795 7

To Michael Bollen –
a friend in need

Contents

Tales from the Labyrinth

The Mourners

True misery

among scattered twigs and earth …

A mouse-wife

in a long cold burrow
deep under the ivy and roots of the bed,

ears, paws folded –

and an old man of the world, far above,
white hair, hands bloody with relics,

bone cold, iron-hard,
held revolving and rigid in an electric field:

stained images
the weird eyes of candles –

in a power-grid of frozen particles …

vanishing down through transfigured night
to a pinpoint-light …

Not a single sleeper stirs
to the terrible cries

as the moon floats down the street

smashing all the windows …

Black Nail Lullaby

If the black nails

aren't hammered in against
        ice-machines of the wind …

if the windows,
        if the doors,

if the broken down-pipes,

– and the fungus-damp,

and the gob-green taps,
and if the pools of grease

and the crap from backed-up sewers,

if the violence,

if another visit from the Welfare,
piece of shite –

cop –

hammer at the door …

                then what couldn't you do, she screamed –
                in a bloodstained nightdress

(rocking backwards and forwards top of the stairs …)

what couldn't you do
with two blue flowers singing like hummingbirds?

Sing Shhh! Shhh!

Shhh! baby Shhh!

Shhh! cold baby,
silent baby in the dark.

With a blue flower in each hand
you can outfly winter ...

Tales from the Labyrinth

Fire!

above Psycho city
        (madmen and children peering through bars
                at forested foot-hills)

where mansions are going under the celestial hammer:

smoke dancing and rolling and laughing …

French pictures –
Sigh of Chinese silk sofas
The sing-song death of grand pianos.

Immolations and conflagrations.

Tomorrow's headlines, TV news
like poetry – like

the soft piping seductions of a distant god

caught in the forcefield
of exploding superhighways

and the purple death-flowers of trees …

Hooligan wolf-masks stare from the clouds.

And lost souls stare up at the action
down in Psycho city,

at a shadow drifting through the mirrors of the Labyrinth,
carrying an empty petrol can,

a vote registered

in a gravity feed of constant oscillations where order and chaos
are alternately smashed into smithereens

by giant red-blue Equalising Machines

and Cosmic Beatitudes …

ONE-TWO!
ONE-TWO!

in the black holes of time.

Forgotten Cyclone Fences

Forgotten Cyclone Fences of the suburbs –
poison pools of acid battery factories

exhaling organic breakdown,

lung-wrack, sulphides and cadaverine –

like dreams flowering again
to become invisible blessed Madonna blossoms

/made whitest white by the purity of death.

Atoms, freed by corruption and sunset-fire collapsars,
fill the sky like a cyclotron.

With blessings of the Exodus – everything is railroaded
to heaven (galvo fences, backyards
lashed by catastrophes, asbestos,

fast-food victims' body parts, factories imploding,
and terrible cancers of the breast –)

In the Church at the Crossroads of the Suburbs,

we baptize all who leave
this cosmic dump – their tongues torn out –

done with suffering, bulldozers, broken glass, screaming anal worms –

we appoint all to rise up in a fistful of shit to be crowned
on the right hand of God the Almighty –

Kyrie Eleison   *Flies in gold vestments blessing all*
with showers of holy and most blessed water among their droppings

Christe Eleison

Like votive candles hanging in a blasted tree,
an unguessable voltage playing at the edge of things –

the graveyard of all souls …

Clone-howl

Where do they come from – these
cruel gene-misfits of the world

(sometimes, there are no hypodermics long enough
to pierce their gluteal-fat)

– They wait patiently, these slowly-gross, immense Earth-Mothers,
in doctors' waiting rooms

a rattling eergh! blll!eergh! of phlegmy tubes …

But sad – so very sad!

Born out of time,
tuberous fingers, squinched-up rosebud lips,

their wasted sprays of cunt-juice, huge clitorises
in steatopygia of the stone-age: paleolithic throwbacks

with inscribed skein-nets of the amniotic
and double-egg buttocks and other metaphors

of the butterfly-charged, cholesterol parts of the Venus…

This once was beauty. O love. O yes! The cellulite. The fecund
of the meat-fed-cave-christened-smoke filthy

big wet tufts of pubic hair. (I love you, caveman! Me too.)

– now leaning on a stick on Underhill, waiting at the bus stop
for the Housing Com. Estate – an eclampsiac

wheezing, adipose drape
of butcher's fat and veins waddling before you at the check-out. ..

or as some smaller mother helps them across the road –

'… take care now!'

Weird shadows from the past, tattooed, the anthropomorphic

reborn into Centrelink records – grotesque dolls, stained sheets
billowing Kmart nightdresses

or engravings in the night-cave of the blood sacred womb
and the dirty streets

with owl-eyes:
old Winged Earth Virgins – waking to aiee-oww-owww
oooaaa aaaa

feathered rush through passage graves

rat-chitter,
moth-glide –

high over the wasteland where false doors open to the Universe

and headless sperm forever circle a low-flying moon …

Gunfire

Sniff gunfire –

mingling death and mysticism in the rain,

50th story up, among Star Force screams,
where a tattooed messiah is being frisked, handcuffed,

face down, between a cooker and a broken table …

Cops lining the stairwell, and neighbourhood denizens –

crowds down in the street, faces like polystyrene

watching concrete crumble around their lives,
as a ponderous block of flats with battlements,

in its quest through time,

detaching itself from a chimney skyscape,
blue neon flashing,

plunges through night again
across the city,

top flats derelict, stairways washed by water …

no destination,
no flag

as it turns screeching into the wind …

just a coloured pin in a map

inherited from long dead police-records …

The Kiss

Now here, now there
I meet them everywhere
in my before-dawn-walks

among Housing Commissiom dreams…

your obsessions and yours,
like soft soup-wisps of drano ghosts
come visiting these exurb streets.

And is it man,
is it woman …?

this last colourless-before-dawn
                    tangling, untangling, mouth-to-mouth

                    KISS

circling about itself

among barf, suck, swill
– the dirtiest love-bite in the universe –

while tongues lollop

like tams-o-bedlam among the sheets:

crippled, neurotic, cognitive dissonances
all come hither to these

earthly joys of crystalline,
and crying for succor in the wilderness –

When – lo!

through dreams,

the moon struggles in a slit of mist, eyes pouring mildew,
a tasseled lampshade on its head,

and arm-in-arm among these emanations that death cannot undo,
we go together up the street,

treading carefully up Venlo, down the Avenue
in before-dawn-light,
from pavement, flag-to-flag,

(*missed a crack*
                    missed a crack!
Step on a crack and break your mother's back)

I like your hat!

(me to the moon)

in the sly intimacy of skid-row friends

The Wish

Deep dark
shot through with brilliant stars of distant Gothic
and flames

where a ring of city faces squat round a fire
in the sense of Picasso clay-workings of flesh-wreck:

tenebrous shadows connected by curling smoke
under the overpass …

    a crackle of phlegm as someone laughs,
    an old woman in layers of salvo,
    a skunk-drunk,
    a glandular hulk …

backed by lumpish silhouette-buildings and the city-moon.

Suddenly a shooting star appears behind a factory chimney

followed by another … light on cheekbones
as an arm-stump flaps in the dark.
Black teeth …

Oooo oooh ah ah ah! (yells the dwarf! the madman?)

With a scream from the old woman … *make a wish, a* … wish
while you can…

and there's another cackle –

segued
by
one
of those moments in the meths-tunnels of time

a rictus of firelit skulls,
eyes closed, clenched up among the blackheads and papier-mâché of the
night ...

..........................*(I only want to be loved:*

No you don't.

........................*Yes I do!)*

.... glimpsed like pieces of paper blowing along a street,

before vanishing upwards
through the eye of a needle.

Whistler

That Black Alzheimer's call – harsh, grating,

crow-like, heavy, sedentary
or locally nomadic:

abandoned sheds, droppings.

Or this – high-pitched, piping –

2nd mortgages,
debt consolidations –

peeling yellow, greyISH-patches,
high in suburban trees, at speed,

(occasional broken gutter-perchers, says the Bird Book)

a morning mist sometimes making identification difficult

between the Lesser Pink-eye
and Dysmcnhorrhoca –

or the Spotted Fever bird and the sneeze-wheeze-haik-haik!
of the Little Snot-Green Dribbler

sighted on rusting traffic lights near Woolies.

(Our members report the initial banding of Chlamidia
was completed April 10th –
Editor)

OBSERVATIONS FROM CUTLAS ST. DERELICT Scout Hut…

include the rarely seen, brilliant scarlet Hymen's Whistler,
C in A-levels Sociology,

a flash of black stockings and a puckered ass-hole –

zipping down Saltfield Rd.,

high over the Wood-Yard
into the wild blue wonder …

The White Cloud

Goodbye to winter – say, chaos! that queer
                                        pox-tat light …

a sudden red-slash across the sky,

as Gunpowder races off –
Spring – a zig-zag fuse spluttering yellow-crimson flowers

across-country roads, over half-buried Council machines,

to explode against the garage door.

And here it rests in the sky,
bottom end of the Estate –
where metal-thrash grunge-disc, dead trees full of venom,

– a copper sheet in the sunset crashes
                                        and flashes glass / glass,
metallic butterflies lift floury antennae,

                                        and red tarmac bubbles
                                        cloud-reflections…

Or – Spring, as in the Taurus glyph, as ruled by Venus:
in the astrological language of the psyche,
                    the womb, fallopian tubes, soft semen,

pubic hairs filling the sink-trap of the universe:

with love / desire /
while, shooting stars zoom

over our 24 hour garage (distant throb) on Main Rd., –
sonic surge – *Def Leppard*
                                        Back to Jerusalem.

And lightning flickers against the blinds.

When, suddenly, 3am the phone rings:

a disturbance in distant Citadels …

bikies and cop-cars parked by a white cloud
                                        high over the Junior School, staring up

at Sid Vicious, dick in hand,
wandering the Milky Way …

Interfacing

So here we are again
interfacing

broadband on a damn weird planet;

double-glazed,
blue gas of distance,

murderously efficient, (it is)

while yet another favourable food-chain crashes through
and Summer flowers
                                        fair seed,
goodfruit –

a Phlegethon of supermarts and talking-fields,
with insect-humm-buzz-whirr

in sweet descent from the clouds on meadow-wings
          and all brands possible of harmonium mundi.

Maybe if this world were kept in a Zip-Lok bag
or the sky a cheap-mirror –

the hopelessly starving and diarrhoeic among the flies and bones
of sub Sahara

could see how nicely our harvest of high protein durum wheat
                                                                 is doing this year.

Or, if they stood on tip-toe in night coming on –
glimpse the pleroma back of the evening star,
in places like

High St., Bumbugger –

where a checkout girl beeps through unending groceries of bloodied flesh
and cream cakes (looking good in nitric acid light)
with this week's giveaway packet of choccy biscuits…

to some waddling obesity

Shadow Play

'Rejoice with me,
For I have found my sheep which was lost ...'

intones the bollocks sheet
outside the Uniting Church:

Friday of the first week in Lent
and this in Marlborough St.,

a warm night
where immigrant dust of Da-Nang and Hue blows past,

coo-ee of closed factories,
by an all-nite caff, a wall spraycanned –

'WHaT TH FuCk about Us ...?'

Waterloo – Landlordland –
working girls in halters and leather skirts.

Like a shadow play viewed through dirty curtains,
acted out by stained effigies

drifting through the dark: the half-mad,
the cruel, the crude – and the witless ...

When a cop car passes,
I watch from the shadows,

And then follow it up the hill
through Nogoland, the demolitions

and St. Luke's, where, lit by occasional
kerb-crawling lights, more shadows lie

wrapped in plastic
and newspaper top of the steps –

in hope of the Resurrection.

A Low Colour-Blast

Wake to a thunderstorm-glow

of a ring-current circling the town

over iron roofs and broken tiles,

        Hear the wind whistling E flat

through thin blue-gray ice of Rimsky Korsakov's
rotting gaps in windowsills,

or Skryabin's purple-violet A flat major
singing round effluents .

Leaking down-pipes
are replaced by new red-blue

colour flashes in storm-black-star windows …

Everytime a colour of lightning or a note vanishes,
another replaces it.

Electric organs, the Clavilux,

Adrian Klein (*Colour Music – The Art of Light 1926)*
writes –

A sequence of lights arranged in logarithmic order
decreasing in intensity is beautiful to witness …
Pure colour, white light, hue, measure and degree,
effected in a predetermined manner etc …

thus, a Language of Light is raised to the dignity of a Fine Art …

Where morning water flows,
gutter-rubbish settling after rain, a puddle-flash

flushes crimson and rainbow-gutter-oil
around orange-rusted cars,

factory windows, wet roads.

At 6 am – blinding, bouncing, colliding-off –

the great colour-streams of the sun seen

through lilac as it licks down through the clouds…

The Mass

Play that medieval organ again
... those puff-ball clouds,

sky-churches,
        cathedrals floating off
into electric fields

and wavelengths – in thousands of billions, White Energy
        pouring through aisles, Divine Light streaming down

        for Palestrina – Choir voices soaring,
suspended, flawlessly constant,

move and counter-move,
        force and contra force,

pure sound,
        pure white light,

        and under it RED
on vestments, people

gazing up to the Red of Heavenly Wounds vibrating
        on the Cross – 750 million-million light vibes per sec.

        flowing down walls, aisles, stickying the fonts
overflowing with terrible salty heat ...

RED
WHITE
RED
WHITE/RED/RED/RED...

Ultrasonic timelines and flowcharts,
bombarded by mediaeval microwave towers of music:

higher and higher,

(Look not, O Lord, upon our sins but the faith of Thy Church)

redemptive wonders, electrifying modern art –

– Thrones and Dominations,
watching amazed through multigrade light,

the awe-flight of basilicas and divine jets zooming away
with snow-choirs and mountains into space and history …

as voices take flight – again – again … *Te deum laudamus* …

(Missa Papae Marcelli circa 1560: Palestrina – legitimate madrigal magic-showman with gargoyles and all the creatures of the Rolling Stones …)

Lonely Planet

A call from the wild where the restless dead range on equal terms,

a moon-flying night bird
which turns and twists
through cloud-souterraines and blank walls
of the past,

its long bitter cry,

head turning this way and that
as it scans the brain-scapes
and attempted poetry

of your life –

Where, dream-by-dream,
it calls you up,
hair and cell from the skull-dead place of sleep,

hair and cell,

through black bursts, rock
and havens
of the mind …

mentor and priest whispering your name

with pale notes on a moonlit hill,

as the down-flying bird
draws
a feather
down the membrane and moon-glass of the town.

When it calls again –

that's desolation.

The Kreutzer Sonata

Goodbye day
farewell flowers …

raw negativity of anguish in Russian winter, stars in conflict,

Pluto's glyph in seething nigredo of the Spirit World
– as a horseman

dismounts in the night, shouting *Da!*

Ice and snow,
the vastness of the country

closes in, footsteps die.

Nothing moves –
Then a far owl-call: rustles of black wind from the Steppes

and branch-whisper…

as a woman screams through dark –

in the forest,
on all fours,

half bird
half ghost

giving birth in the undergrowth: gouts of black blood
with hair and filth:

on all fours screaming as she gives birth to death:
birth through Tolstoy, death through Tolstoy's

long silent look through the cosmic wilderness of Ludwig B's twilit soul.

There in the night. This is the moment of final obsession.
The dagger in and convulsing.

Strong adult themes, a hex of bloody notes spilled from an empty violin
case –
a severed wigless head staring through iron and clouds ...

Li Shizheng Moves House*

Hearing mice in winter, dim, cold time,

he has loaded
his furniture on a cart –

leaving only his outline
crouched, snarling in the plaster;

now he moons in an earth closet
blood-red with the wasted eggs of his wife,

watching, as she takes the half-dark
like a wide brush

to paint herself in the Past, her beautiful throat
singing in another life …

And he wades out across the mud …

Goodbye, goodbye!

Joining the columns as they move along, legs heavy
as plum trees, bent double –

hundreds of millions, the Dim Black Star of Creation
shining from their foreheads,

millimetre-by-millimetre as they shuffle along
through the yellow clay,

balancing the Mainland of China
on their shoulders,

while the rivers flow backwards …

*　　　　　　*

Bones torn apart,

skulls attached by lengths of string:

Spring, a golden bird in a blue bamboo basket,
sings over a municipal dump covered in snow...

as a farm horse gallops past,
its face a mask of blood —

and two oxen silently drag a coffinwood plough
around the world..

*   *

Meanwhile, over duck and champagne in the city,
the swanky nouveau-riche discuss the mysteries
of fatty acids, proteins, cholesterol, total trans-saturated ...

and what can be done about it?

* Penname Duoduo: born 1951. A pre-and-post Tiananmen poet.

Shanghai flash

An auspicious dynasty, Chinese Microsoft eyes
diving through

a blood-gas sky –
ocean of export days,

howl ghost-like through emporia of the world,

tossing lives like washing machines
and laser paper

while skyscrapers roar back –

A gargantuan *heave!*

bowling the laughing wind-monsters off
down the street

where they scoop dripping foam
from puddles

with their long, curved Mandarin claws.

(a wailing of iron flutes and *suo na,*
Old Warmasters from hell beating ghost drums

beyond The Wall)

Only to materialise again outside the Shanghai Bank today.

A sudden dazzle-dazzle!

Spotless glass doors opening for a spirit in search
of three beautiful young wolves

who have recently attained human form,

are caught in the *zing-a-ling of a Feng Shui mirror,*
where the demon whirls

becoming a flash of crystal

chiming-squares,
triangles entering sudden melt
of blaze-blue-diamond ...

another of the many Sun Creatures

from Li Chin's Book of Changes...

Coming Down

China Railways

coming down —

Main Liner QJ,

black smoke,

bringing flowers, food and hell-money
for Quing Ming, Autumn Moon;

Jagged Peaks,
Snow North:

Silk Scarves,
The Great Wall and Fighting Battlements

it drags behind ....

A QJ 2-10-2, draped with pink cantaloupes
and doom-cities, coming down

from Badaling

through breeze-block suburbs,
can tear the trashgates of your heart wide open ...

High noon,
hot breath,

and pure wax ghosts:

billowing *hisss!clouds!Slow! Huge*
moist- silk-strokes of Sex/Power/Sex/ Power-power...

S.L.O.W.I.N.G.

The Eternal Pavilion of Ten Thousand Happiness

floating on a Butterfly Wind ...

Puppets

God!

(Cagney! Stallone!)

this is
for *you*,

God!

I'm glad they killed *yr.* son …

People, deformed gnomes,
puppets snarling through

a haze of Y chromosomes.

Skulls dance in the wind – Bong! Bong!
It's the iron-churchbell for Punch…

No redemption outside the hangman's rope!

– they'll slice and dice
– they'll burn his bones until he moans …
– he'll die a fifty thousand coloured cockroach death!

This is for you, bastards! – Punch with 'plastique'
strapped to his body,

Punch dancing on the corpses of his tiny stage,
Punch cursing God, the politicians, the filthy streets,

Punch miming the Devil's Trill on his machine pistol
– a demonic fiddle-strings moment

drilled through sapstain
and wood to cleave the mountain

and destroy the sky-wild calyx in the sun …

Somewhere, a Fixer in a Kevlar vest lurches down a doomed street –

and blood-splashed puppets in a field of violets and snow,
caught in the forcefield of a Stradivarius,

stare up through weaving / interweaving skeins,

at the jerking, working Showbiz strings
of the Smiling Puppet Master's Theatre of the Macabre,

lights, bells, jingles / serial-killer-movie library of the Universe…

The Cake

A terror-strike sweeps in
(mixed with the rotor-katter-chatter-katter of chopper-gunships)

turns tight and Uies in shatter / roar
of mammoth-mask domination, buildings' implosion

and dream sequences textured with
dawn-vortex-fire sweeping

down a Palestinian street.

Among the rubble of a kitchen, a soldier later picks up
a recipe and a neighbourly cake is baked –

being iced with a flamethrower …

and turning gold,
absolute 22 ingot,

the tomb of Abraham, opening and closing with flowers –

as it starts to rotate / faster / faster …
flashing like an astral sphere
lit by 10,000 Menorah.

And everyone in the bomb-shelter closes their eyes and makes a wish.

Happy birthday, Hamas …

(Hezbollah)

The Butterfly Effect

a / h
h
h …

a spindrift
barely exhaled,

a blue shadow slowly crossing an aquamarine lake,
flowering karma in the infinite flow of time –

But who sees the butterfly leave …?

The World turns,

– fabulous creatures of the winged
antirrhinum and day-lily,

spirals of sukta and mandala,
the void vertigos

into faintest tap-tap of a distant hammer.

Then a lake of frogs vanishes …

miles away –
a river of drowned animals…

Or nearer home, in wind-chaos lashed by green willow,
mad-anima of poison minds

dream again Orgasmatron,
Massive Noise Injection

in third world village killing grounds…

People sleeping / not / in a coma of souls,
children in stone dugouts, stunned,

stare up through black poetry stronger than heaven,
the belly-up moon lit by

blue/purple Fleshgrinding Flash of B52 bomber-Destiny
further down the Valley –

deafened by the Huge Galaxy of Murderbox…

Murderbox 10

shouting – *they're dead!*
they're dead!

Nothingface

Demo-time sets your watch

flashing
black
bullet-proof

scizophrenia/phrenia
threat/double-threat –

All Sundayprime crime time
in the half life of uranium,

escalators hang motionless
between planets: banners far off /

shouts of a mob embroiled ...

Smoke rises. Clocks tick.

Nothingface stares from the sky:

the Big + + + Ambulance Church on the hill –

'... get away from Me you unclean,
    you incestuous tribes of Baal...'

as tall fire-engines on immensely thin prehensile legs
rush through the city

shrieking

Fahrenheit Red!
Fahrenheit Red!

On the way to the hospital –

Traffic Priests, tall Pharaohs
in Glitterland,

cop cars embroidered with flowers
and acid bird-masks

bar the way.

In the lift to the thousandth floor
                    six / Butterfly ghosts
                    w/ blood-soaked wings

en route from history on these shores
to a Parallel Universe

The Trap

So bless us all – we witnesses to her beat

through God's Country behind the Footy Ground,

up Centrelink Boulevard,
down Virulence,

Mrs Bleedinglegs, ulcer-veins and crutch,
has picked

– FantaCoopers7upCokeOrangeLemon
                SpriteSpritzSnotopPepsiCoolers!

Bins and dumpsters rifled – say, 100 + tinnies flattened
and a dozen bottles to the trolley,

moving slowly – step by step –
back and forth –

until this sunset snugs her down,

corner

of the Recycling Depot

where the bus shelter, the trolley and she
fly nightly through wormholes in the curve of time –

Sleeping children look up in moonlight:

                '… good on you, bless us! Mrs Bleeding Legs!' they shout,

Madmen with black breath wave, swans
fall through dead-wax into silver

and slime-birds peck at the lilac eyes of fish.

Her leg, a thin pole with dirty bandages
sticks through a broken window …

while the half-moon with dirty fingernails,
watches from the roof of Jeb's Bankrupt Sales,

    dog
            eating dog
            eating dog
            eating shite –

on a planet struggling in
in the last pure glass Sky Crap-Trap of the Universe …

The Sheds

As Autumn waves goodbye! –

a caprice of carmine slashes the mist,

and lights! we dance! they scream,
        because we are eternal –

        A wag of torn webs in platinum and dead flies
where ghosts present *you*

with a filled vase and purple die-back,
the smell of rot among heavy nerves, the short-arsed first,
the macro-cephalic at the back

with helping of mordant grief.

All night, phylacteries of sex-dreams
and wet leaves blows under the door. A window bangs

and *you* wake to self-transcendence, the soul made flesh
with disembodied hands in cold glass

        between your legs.

I'm here, you scream to the dark
as it wavers across the floor –

now love me for myself…

But dreams cramp on nothing: aborted babies
burrow inside you,

turning this way and that, pissing into your bladder
and leaving their rubbish behind:

you can hear them beating on their tiny soles
with little sticks of death while garbage bins

clatter off down the street,
and giant snails keep eco planet-watch

between moonlit sheds,

crawling through star-lit time
then vanishing atom-by-atom

among the stars.

Curr. Vitae

It happens through the last dream of birds singing:

an exordium of mind-crystals

are suddenly, extraordinarily pulled out among the harmonics

by waahga – waaha – gaga

foulbreath
bloodsuck,
dentures under the pillow, the black soul in a faceful of mouth-swill,

And the dream become a man just dumb-dozing in the scratcher,
half-an-ear to doors slamming and water flushing

(morning in these damn thin walls of the Universe)

as gray light waits for the first flash-flash
of the Dow Jones
and the tap-tap- of hammers erecting today's Centrelink slogan over High St. –

Arbeit Macht Frei

with municipal baskets of flowering assholes down the Mall
which loathly ope' their brilliant eyes …

O world happiness! first blue collar traffic!
and ghosts of street-works!
Where kids still lie in their ammoniac gear, gob-faces caked with snot …
and last dreams exit their mouths with screams from underground gaspipes

The exhilaration! The blood-surge as another day invades the curtains

with overcast swirling through the skankydrift
and, distantly, a blackbird grates out a whistle on a hidden wire:

Un moment musicale – a PS to add to your curric. vitae
as your foot collects another kiddy fecal-wipe

on the way to the lav

Play Zoom

Enlivened by strokes and varicose veins,
low-end Valium Nursing Homes

dive this way/that

through clouds of black bacteria –

play zoom-play-zoom!

In windy patter of rain down The Avenue,
winter clatters bolts and tiles, last leaves:

steam rises from paraffin-ringworm baths,
hip-hop-hap … old incontinence and cabbage,

and won't eat,
can't eat,

caper, caper, caper
upstairs/down ...

(tied to their chairs,
the games old people play)

But the Mammoth Master's
Ghostbuster Wings are everywhere …

flapping down long corridors, through iron doors' unexpected openings
into Alzheimer-icy blasts between 2 worlds,

faces eaten by weird and doom
forever lost and never found in dark clouds over the town.

Where old people, frail as glass, peer out over snowy gulfs, clutch
barred windows, mouthing

into radio station brrr-brrr!

whispered telephone calls –

Play Someone to Look Over Me
Play In the Blue of the Evening

Play I believe …
                                        in the Resurrection
                                        and Life Everlasting…

Scroll

For Pat and Ron Newlands

And especially for you now – this touch of night
with enriched scallops of sulphides: where the moon
over the Freeway

slides its butter-knife

among cloud-under-pearled by clouds

and a lean-necked bird screeches
by a dripping overflow with a scissor-beak clack!

– And wings take air (long paddle-legs in wet dabble thrust
against night-spirits of black waters) far cry
circling the town sewage filter-ponds …

and, again, high over the Trailer Park,
Woolworth's and Bi-lo

where the moon picks out a silhouette – black on white /
drifting chemicals in total lacklustre …

'Lone Bird, Long Journey over High Chimneys …'

in greasy-fume

long-distance
diesel-gloop
brush strokes

a humble scroll by Zhang Lu for the Emperor of Yoggins

and his starry soldiers

so coldly nailed over this Freeway Night.

Lift-off, son!

Listen to that weird singing *in excelsis – very thin and high*

among multi-sky scrapers, vitreous curves,
tinted mirror-glass:

where flute- winds echo from one
void to another

through rectilinear homogeneities–
with hidden voltages

crackling at the dangerous edge of things …

Oil, surreal chemicals, the genome factor.

Futuramas –

whispering echoes of all-shock genius
and distances our children cross

like strangers rocketing a billion miles between aeons
of gobsleaze and intergalactic business mayhem – as in

Fortunate Escape from the Planet of the Apes, dad!
Or – my brilliant career in Geneva with Stock Options ..

Moneymarket's parallel universe for digital star-busters'

piggy-back into history from back kitchens, worn carpets;
through love-smashed gene-horizons –

rocket-jets blast a silent arc over blanked-out towns
and glimmering street lights at night

We have lift off
lift off …

(daddy)

Levers / Lights

Pack *The Equations of Everything* –

and all the days' virulence and distillate of humanity
into one enormous Tycoon Power Box:

Power = Levers = Overload:

lights

flashing / King Glo Company bases

spasming out ocean-flows of computer-figures
and ultra Elysium / ultra Effluvium

through van de Rat's Land:

… trust your accountants,
    let the wind carry you – writes the poet

– of that dank blank,
– that face of facelessness,
    vanished into

    Part 9. 4 Division I Corporation Law,
    Specific Offences …

    or buried in the chanting of night vigils
    by the black autopsy of lost souls …

From the wild borders of tomorrow

whose vast conurbations are interred under
violet clouds of Polystyrene and Factor X –

O Blessed Mathew, speed-reader
of dodgy balance sheets … with Jesus,
the Three Buddhas, patrons of decaying Utopias

and fast food particles –

pity these dumb creatures of the void

stumbling through a Tupperware Biosphere –

and the dead – high
on a substance so terrible –

it has no name …

Anti-sleep

The world's shrinking.
It whispers through the quantum encrypted schizophrenia

of blood & snot in Glitterland.

... Primary vibrations,
  and anaphylactic shock

with syndicated howls
melding anti-sleep

and the gross systolic-diastolic-machine-squeals
of history.

It drifts among the stars. Globalisation with hissing vents –
an iron nodule drifting through clouds of c. dioxide,

plumes of pharmaceuticals
and GM in tail-gating traffic

over pot-holed roads,
past broken-backed factories: the gape of Chinese squats

And a sign pointing – *New York 2 miles*
London – follow the big plastic footprints...

It rolls

through the capitals of sleep, a hopelessness
in a world vanishing between the cry of lost souls
caught between the nano-world of the Matrix

and the roar of rusty iron pushing up through the soil.

When the laws of destiny and physics
make the world small enough to fit in one hand

(or a metal ring to wear on your finger
and all happiness is America-shaped …)

                              maybe someone
will chalk a black circle round it

forever.

Another Frontier

He's a p-puppet bobbing,
b-b-bobbing

almost under the zzcch-splash! twenty wheeler's
bullbar at the traffic lights:

– an all-muscle-truckie's stare

at a dwarf triple-cripple

blown over the crossing –
wave of a twisted hand,

a splay-leg dragging
the other, head-lolling-chimp-grinning / Rain /

where a Lone Tree whips, slashes at the squall.

And still dancing at the next inter-section …

a splash through sudden-dazzle-showrooms
gold dishlex, hoover,

shop-shock!

brings him a laughing-lurch between traffic.

Exploding sun triangles on chrome
flash-blind-happy

vanish, reappearing /

showdown between optic laser-monsters
and shining death-ray warriors

of brain lesions,

another frontier …

Briars

After the shop-jock of cheaper prices and Woolworth lights –

        (against the backdrop of grot-lacklustre,
hole-in-the-wall public urinals)

the winter light shifts again;

a roof-shimmer edges into green-olive-drab
and breeze-block-gray becomes very faint cancer-violet.

Down Marlborough , past the Sip n' Save with my shopping,
I also suss-out the swelling secret of the briar-rose

which towers over
the Electric Factory's tall cyclone fence:

– whose dire thorns, having fastened
into the soft phlegm of existence, their private infra-red beams
now scan the flash-tak of Industrial Murder—

bip-babip-bip-bip

the Infant School, the Car Wreckers Inc.
and the whole rotting infrastructure of cold-water rentals.

While briars sway, green-sharp among

this general ambience of the unlovely,
sun lights the parked rust-traps,
and the distant sound of kids singing la-la-la etc.

in the fantastic-angelic of first primers –

– all it needs now
is a single brilliant instance of the Birth Passage –

one rose of Spring

to tilt the neighbourhood.

Ciggie

Where crazed parolees
and roses bloom in the cracks of our Lost City,
estate kids are raising hell,

and Thin Legs is killing time by the front gate
with Bouffant Dirty Hair …

Shouts rise:
a spotty dog dances, barks
at a bare-arsed toddler, kitten-in-arms,

crouching for a pee.

An intimate neighbourhood scene, in which –
as a Council house-painter might squint,
head back, top of his ladder,

before adding a final touch to an architrave,

or a lead-guitarist suddenly bite-in over the keyboard,
shattering the strobes –

so Madame Bouffant,
without interrupting her flow,
seizes the moment by taking a final drag at her ciggie –
and, with the casual artistry of the 40-a-day-er,

flicks her butt over the squatting child,

shower of sparks in the gutter,
a split second before
a trickle of yellow piddle

douses it.

The Stone Lions

A sudden wind …

in quick flurry of the invisible
passing the Church-in-Demolition,

becoming a vortex,

swerves back of the butcher and the florist shops,
a whirl of papers, dust, flower petals,
                opening its cloak of powdery dogshit

to reappear as the Alley Princess, Queen of Rubbish
and Rotten Bones spinning in a mysterious form.

A veil of flies circles the sun.

And people drift off through the mirage.

Cracked lions on stone plinths
roar over the Church …

Our Lady of Being Fucked-up and The Abused Child's Aaaah! …
of the Bloody Needle
and Rotten Morning-Breath –

early heat that strikes from the tarmac, flies /
and it's all one
                – part of all that abides – today, flashed-colours,
                this *now* of rubbish, papers from the chippy

filling the mouth with grit-tatty-phlegm –

in yet another filthy / sacred poem of the streets /

hung-over in the dusty light …

The Statue

Even their snap *
                                        was weighed;

a miner's wife broke wind, it was written down.

Anything for a book! †

He danced,
alleys, black streets, hovels …

knocking on doors,
making scrawly notes

Heel-and-toe,
here-a-crack, there-a-crack,

his face sparkled like the sun,
his smile was blinding orangeade with Fantablasts
and collared shirts …

I love you all, brothers! he spruiked,
                                                  arm waving, gangly-bowing,
and very evangelical-tall.

Old Etonian, ex-Colonial-anti Semite-cop, aka Blair –
George Orwell was of another set

to whom *past was never prologue* –
                                        whose class fed on social history
                                        like the soft ganglia of the dead **   opining later –

'... there's a lot of rot talked about the sufferings of the working class. I'm not so sorry for the proles myself. Did you ever know a navvy who lay awake thinking of the sack? The prole suffers physically – but he's a free man when he isn't working... ***

Once, in the roller-coaster of time, back of an Orwell picture
I came on a small 1935 poem

viz –

Ugh! Yaach's gray-greasy stink
jew- finger-slip. Slime,
and horror-dudes'
stained buttocks unpretty ooze.
Stomp!

Scream! Stomp! Scream!

A literary paranoiac who will be remembered

as a ghost digesting its own skull
while lurching through black mirrors of Auschwitz

in death's drear kingdom, hissing *Anarchist*! *Socialist!*

– or as any racist, pre-McCarthy class-bigot is remembered,

hard-wired in utero

with twisted anima:

a stained-concrete-tongued statue in the Park
among all the flowers of people passing by ...

* Food
† *The Road to Wigan Pier* ** *Animal Farm* *** *Coming up for Air*

Oranges and Lemons

The Bristol Downs. Sunday:
(for Margaret, Gwin, Annie, and Belinda)

Past England's closed factories – rush of clouds,
and diesel fumes –

past faraway landscapes
drip-drip of rhododendrons, rolling lawns,

high over Sheraton and Hepplewhite Houses
faintly ring the Sunday bells …
By oriel windows, Queen Ann,

Stockbroker-Tudor,

the Lake, the Summerhouse …

W.E'V.E > N.E.V.E.R > H.A.D> I.T > S.O > G.O.O.D

spruik the bells
of St Glee …

D.E.E > D.E.E > D.E.E > D.E.E >

(and ever further and mistier into coppices of Oak and Beech)

Ashlar and freestone, Anglican steeples,
transepts, towers and spires –

or echoing nearer over birch and monkey puzzle,
by cul-de-sacs,

multi-car garages and swimming pools,
the golf course and the pony club –

bells broad, shoulders squared,
sound-bows thick rah-rah out among country clubs

W.E > M.U.S.T. >K.E.E.P > I.T > L.I.K.E > T.H.I.S

peal the bells
of St Whatsis …

Around ferned-and-fountained gardens of the Council Estates
and the Whitelady squats …

– From gable-ends to Gothic Pine:

you can't get closer to God than this…

Honey

…now a swerve up over blackberry hordes
   and the disused railway

where flies-through morning light,
a sky-touch with chords of benediction:

past earthworks, guts and cables
of the world laid bare, sewer pipes,
the electricity sub-station …

on the bees forage: gray Carniolans, drones:

up Dunkirk, Alamein,
the gardens from hell, flowers lea of dogshit,

smashed carboys on the Wasteland,
piles of concrete …

Horehound and Scabious,

each blue-and-old gold to hold like flambeaux
against the dying of the light …

Top end of the estate, from the backdoor of
her crazy boardhouse, an old bee woman,

one arm like a withered antenna,
sells the sweet dark honey-stuff

treasured from the mother-lode of earth

in jars scavenged from the rubbish dump.

So it's a trash neighbourhood.

Who cares?

Christmas Eve

A last piercingly sweet Hallelujah-shriek of the blue-glass Virgin
as a final nail is hammered in through The Crib

and some bastard snatches the after-birth …

Now the world will be saved
through the mysterious union of blood

and the throb-throb pounding of the Corporate Sector's

Complete-Self-Injecting-Dream-Machine Inc.

– lost streets where strips of orange polystyrene blow,
needle-stick dogs howl,

and Intergalactic Plastic Xmas Tree Flames
sweep up high and glittering over the Tabernacle choirs

among deafening Tinsel-Factories thundering away:

the madness of clowns, cemetery-clouds

drifting along Ground Zero, past Woolies,
struck blind by balloons and prisms in Cheap-as-Chips …

Adeste Fidelis / laeti triumphantes …

… in the gaudy lives of angels and hymn books,
white bacteria / flashing at the speed of light.

The Shelter

… where the gene pool,

whirlpool
colour-swirled up the street
last night …

now two carved hearts beat on a stunted tree
behind the footy ground

he/ loves me!
he / loves me! not!

Neighbourhood screams and shit,
exhaust fumes
and OK dirt of everyday:
will cover the sun

before their story's told.

But today it's their tree,

the pageantry,
the electrophoresis …

It's the first day of Spring,

it's a morning like this when the world
– born and re-born

glints on glass and weeds –

a blitz of sunbeams—
confetti-tickets at the Greyhound Stop …
and it's now and forever!

By a vandalised bus shelter

beside cold grease litter of remnant takeaways,
used toilet paper, and broken bottles –

a baby's echo-cry from a passing pram
                                        trails through the air

waving and flowering
on a tall blue stem …

Sleepers

Black shadows,
then the light …

tonal variations in a tangle of wet streets

and shutter speeds: *looking for the single interpretive statement*:

an X-ray through rotting wood,
closed factories …
locked church on the corner –

and the Hostel of All Souls.

Behind hunched, fitful chiaroscuro,
wind-soughing shrubbery – from what was once prime estate –
rain water runs from broken down pipes,

a cloud-swept atmospheric lead-in
to a shot by Nitelight

about 2 a.m. in a Salvo room of sleeping men:

a Pentax 35 mm Ektachrome 160,
light of the moon down the goiterous throat

of an old dosser with rotting teeth.

Click!

The wind: cold phantasmagoric, like kissing
the lymph glands of the dead,

while dreams form in nude-swirl and mega-colour,
and broken factory glass flash moon! moon!

Flushed by halitosis –
it arches up over the power stacks and the hallelujah void

while the street flies round the city, gently shaking its tambourine.

Blow the trumpet! to the power and glory …
to the power and glory

Blow the trumpet to all these shadow-creatures sliding by.

The Old Man

Blending lime-lilac with distant echo-streets,
the lone SunSnake's silent
glitter-coil wraps

roofs of the closed Small-Goods Factory
with blue-grey zones of loneliness and silence.

Hard by, distant traffic sounds
and far-away shunting from the Railway Yard:

in Baker Place, a sleeping figure hunches
over the steering wheel of a car up on bricks,

and small alley-butterflies
flutter-arc-fluttering around the bins –

Suddenly, an event: a whirlwind forms, tossing grit

and rubbish into the air …
then goes to sleep again –
a moment observed

by a cat
on the wall,

a beetle
emerging from a
milk bottle

and

an old man
                                        by the back-door

in a wooden chair –

all staring into the 21st Century

Wind-fade

… of course, infant dayhowls,
torn psyches –

the sun's,
quick dazzle blind-white
shadows

– toyland

children staring up into the sky:

> '… are you happy,
> dum dum dum
> tra la la
> dee di doh …'

Voices come and go, vanishing into wind-fade.
Then a blackbird calls,

glides from a rhododendron,
hops fretfully on the path,

before whisking off to perch among
the others – the rotting, the gap-toothed graves
of the elders –

the ancestors,
vanished into the serenissima, the matrix –
where all is a waiting calm …

not these chaotic black energy night-clusters,

cries, and half-toothed wailing under clay-tonnage
behind the church,

weird feast of infant bones in the jaws of life.

Apostate Sunrise

Vivid butchery! Splashed! Apostate! Bloodswill-window!

And Zola's black cloud-finger
pointing through
the curtains

J' accuse!

That

AH!

of Awe –
all that sweet-sacred-sun's red religious wax
dripping

between chimneys …

god-drunk

Rebus of the Trinity
Jewel in the Sperm of the World

that radiant-moment,
Dharma of Time,
shivering violin-petals at sunrise

when an armful of

world roses,

Meilland/Iceberg,
falls slowly over the junction of Wellington Rd.

and the Freeway North …

(among car-factory-windows gashing black-purple / amazed /
back-signalling – blood puddles,

gut-red over the Job Centre and the Railway Yards,

– you'd think only an ordained priest
could have so much power over the human soul)

Monkey…

Equivocation.
The tail-end of a dream,

– this knell-doubt-knell,
tocsin at the soul's iron gate

– dire sounds of rebuttal and surrebutal.

Concept, judgment, argument and method –
– or being lucky as a Vatican monkey
(glimpsed top of the tree

in a bookshop window – robes, age spots, the famous Ratzinger grin)

that wakes you, heavy skinned and greasy,

– your life confronted by the maugre of
a wordless cry echoing round the world –

bastards! You pope ghosts! I didn't ask to be born, did I…?

Last toot-toot of liberation theology or whip-poor-will casuistry
from the wasted years…

It circles your head like the Curia.
Like the Sacred Congregation of the Faith.
A poison-whisper

in an irony of time waiting for a meniscus trembling on a distant star.

Or, at 3 am – holding a copy of your own *Apologia pro Vita Sewage,*

you could always pick up a cushion,
sit in an empty bath,

and laugh while you cut your face off …

The 1812

Pyotr (Illyich) Tchaikovsky – known to the Central Committee

(favourably) for his fever wall-to-wall … *Waaah!*
fuck you! Eternal Empire Doom,

Spirits of Fiery Winter Palaces sprayed from enormous trumpets …

all Kremlin-to-Kruschev echoing to that glory-mush,
human eyeballs, horses slithering towards the Dnieper,

– to the death dreams and disembowelments of violins,
the cannonade of I-spy, the rat-packs of soldiers –

because there was no end to Tchaikovsky's funky-fury:

Tchaikovsky in a sailor-suit; Tchaikovski who'd never known death …
but jazzed-up death to make the most beautiful

rainbows of aaaagh! skeletons gaping

ever jived from the mouths of musical instruments.

Shostakovich would have washed out his mouth
with green soap – and kicked him downstairs:

'… bug on you for an immature aristocratic fuck-ears!'

Dmitry Sh. who lived through war-siege Leningrad
and knew green death creeping through cellars

with its poisonous fug –

who flew round the world like an archangel,
his eyes lasering symphonies from the rock and tears

of the planet – this power-soul
who wept for the Cosmos –

would rather have walked through a world of broken glass.

He'd rather have put on the clothes of silence
and become a tree …

China

For Adela May

'The Five Towns'– words spoken with the flat-blat
of the Midland's nesting in thick smoke,

136 tons of coal to the firing – giant hourglasses
propped against a metaphor

and tip-tilted

in a vortex of cobbles, factories and black bottle-kilns
sucked up into all the flame-poison-hiss

urban frontier of the barren lands …

Where the scene flips into –

Minton, Shelley, Worcester, Coalport –
with faint cantillations of the dead,

whispers of poison gases in bisque ovens –

and this most beautiful translucent ware held
against the light in which moons forever circle

a single diffuse source of energy in pearl-black space.

Fantasia of pierced vases, Japan sprays,
an Infant Christ, a Charbonnier…

bronze, gilt, pâté- sur- pâté, lustre and Intarsio

and in the museum of time –
among the role-call of thousands:

George Owen, Harry Stinton, F. Rhead! Modelers, painters –
Harold Austin, on whose paintings butterflies would land:
Davis (Dummy) gilder, born deaf and dumb.
Harry Davis, foreman painter; father Alfred, a china presser,
his grandfather Josiah, a fine painter
Stella Crofts, lame, bone TB, signed work in many Museums:
T. Everett, painter of fine flowers – became blind etc...

I also name the bastardy of those low-wage towns –
crucible of night-sweats
that sucked the oxygen from the air

and monstered everything before it in a giant pack
of graveyards and sewer-pipes ...

To these – as the son of smoke
and sperm of blue-star-china, I offer this poem –

high on sunset ridge / over the chimneys,
a worker's done- life
mindless buzz
slobber-slit-throat-work bench ...

in a golden picture tilting from the wall of the universe ...

Baby

… Gestalt malignancies:

Tycoon-Ubermensch screams from the Sacred Temple in the wood
as faux colours flood to the spot

where ageing flesh is born and reborn.

– Surreal test-tube bandages

in stem cell / organ implants dreaming clone-immortality
where it circles a giant Wurlitzer flashing

Reichstag …
Reichstag
Reichstag

With foetal fantasies,
millions upon millions,

wriggling nuclei,
giant fontanels:

        (territory of the quick medical billion,
                slaughterhouse themes with smoke
        billowing from Faustian-devil eyes)

– But hist! that Golden Door inscribed with mystic signs,
those weird energies filter-sucked

through a haze of gas and nutrients – code of the Masked Hand
tiptoeing around Ectomorphs and Hirudoids
among the unkillable ripples of Disneyland, secretly trying out

one beautiful Genome Key after another
in the Insane Temple of the Ageing Surreal.

Deep in the Sacred Wood and the unborn, –

arm-in-arm
among the flowers,

Nietzsche and Wagner

singing

Ego-ego/the Epic cont'd ...

Is it true love, in the rectum ? / My waking
was a kind of sleeping…
Sam Beckett

Hi! I! I!

Me
Me
Me – echoic archetypal voice from the past …

Ego-ego!
slow to materialise through the steam …

the yodeller in the bathroom mirror tries again –

ME!

MEMEMEME!

Singing, fluorescing – a merry mouille
of lips writhing in squidlike squabble with itself:

a spatulate finger inserted into the mustachioed, mucus-lining
of the cheek – suddenly snaps back

pop-BANG! spray of saliva onto the mirror …

an Odyssean Nose
blows space sludge into a handkerchief.

Hello! Hello world!

What changes, what tech. miracles for the Universe
in ten billion years …

Hello…
Hellolololo! It's ME! I've MATERIALISED!

MEMEME! O!O!O!O! YES!YES!YES!YESSSS!

Suddenly, a computer-screams …… RED crossbones/crossbones
FLASHES!!
!!!! AN ILLEGAL OPERATION HAS BEEN PERFORMED…

vanishes into Planck's Constant,

earth drops into sun, sun
liquifies into buckyballs, electrons and Schrodinger's cat,

as Molloy / Ego/ego, a spirit of reiterate divinity,
simultaneously ejected from the gazillionth floor
of Hotel Non-Coding — like Perceval ,

Shape Changer with alchemy of ruefulness,
Christian in his eternal quest among The Vanities
of Weltanschauung for Self and rebirth

in the House of Gathering – sets forth again
through blazing Zodiacs lit by weird dissonances in Time

and vain civic pride:

Wanderer of the Grail, Angel of Dumb Fire in worlds
without meaning, the Twelve Instant Mix Pillars of Wisdom

and the Hundred Mirrors of Silence

with Merlin Eek! and weird Buckyball dance/blitz
forever and relentlessly

(Ah! Strange once-upon in the bathroom mirror! among broken tongues
of the bed, still lost in the insane poetry of sky-jubilee)

and all the Voodoos of the Walking Dead …

Wakefield Press

The Stone Ladder

Peter Lloyd was born in the English Midlands and emigrated to Australia in the late 1970s. Most of his working life has been dedicated to providing housing for the under-privileged. He lives in the Adelaide Hills and is married with two children. Peter has had work published in Australia, Canada, the United States, the United Kingdom and France.

… in Peter Lloyd's hands, outrage at our blasted and despoiled world is turned into lightning-shafts of poetry.
J.M. Coetzee

The palette of a lifetime: powerful, achingly mature and enormously entertaining.
Stephen Lawrence, *Wet Ink*

A master craftsman. I can't remember the last time I encountered such seamless technical ability in an Australian poet.
Justin Lowe, *Thylazine*

Head and shoulders above the rest.
Glen Murdoch

By the same author

Black Swans (1997)

Collage (2002)

A Fingerpost for Rembrandt (2004)

The Stone Ladder

Peter Lloyd

Wakefield Press
1 The Parade West
Kent Town
South Australia 5067
www.wakefieldpress.com.au

First published 2008

Typeset by Michael Deves, Lythrum Press, Adelaide
Printed and bound by Hyde Park Press

ISBN 978 1 86254 795 7

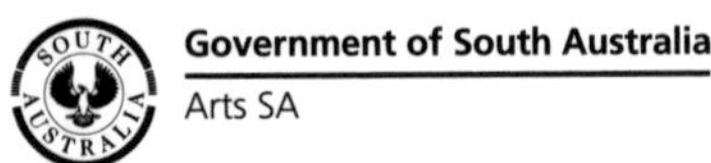

To Mark and Liberty –
and my grandchildren Cate, Aidan, and Toby
with all possible love

Contents

The Stone Ladder

Contents

The Stone Ladder

Teeth

Where three household rubbish bags
tossed from a passing ute,

to burst like bombs on landing,

now sculpt themselves against a lamp post
with gloomy grume of the ignoble,

rancid gloop,

among assorted bottles, rags, takeaways – in which –

by freak of the artistic,
4 decomposing kittens
are arranged

in a tableau of the violently disposed:

viz. one, in hope and prayer of the Resurrection, staring at the void,
two locked in mop-and-bucket grip to the death,

and the raging other,

eyeless-with-maggots, spitting and rampant on an empty can,
but still out there among the metaphysics –

teeth bared like rat-puke
as it
waits
the next
turn

of the Cosmic Wheel / flawed universe / fork in time

as it applies right now ...

Curtains

The dream ends

when the Ghost-bird calls;
dry leaves and twigs blow through a room

– a moment where time drifts –

and I wake, head on my dead wife's breast,

shouting –

'Thief! Give me back my life …'

Her eyes are blue, wide open in the dark,

and the curtains billow.

But it's only time sliding back into the Archives …

The Orange Mist

Bog standard typeface of a town that's vanishing –
with most sorrowful winds off the Pier…

Closed warehouses,
gantries out of work

as waves' thunk-tup,
washing rubbish in through the dark,

tup-thunk among rotting wharves –

and an orange-rust mist
rolls through the silent town – over the abandoned viaducts

and this midnight in the Well of Souls,

this sad-sod mute Kingdom Come (of *when the oil runs out,*

when the coal, the lead, the aluminum, when all the crap has gone
and earth dongs like an old iron ball)

– a moment when guard dogs in empty factories
snarl at ghosts in the street and the ultimately iced

she-body of the moon moves cloudily

and cellar
to attic,

wives
shhh!

sleepless! scrub...
scrub through the night

faster,
faster,

but the strange orange mist is everywhere

it's in the dream, it's in the beds --

and it's eating
the house up.

they can hear lions roaring ...

The Naked Wife

To hear them at night – the familiars,

put your ear to her belly

and listen to the faint click of tiny bones
and pelvises creeping in,

generations between the moonlit sheets

getting their feet under the table
through the slit wet door,

parting her legs,

moist hairs creeping wider

in the complete silence of the groping sperm,
and its blind excreta –

a blue star shining in the middle of her forehead …

Readings from Exodus

In which
the stars are frost,

and the silver Christ,
(sky-lighting the world over Woolworths,
Bi-Lo before dawn)

hovers over a sleeper,
curled on newspapers –

touching him on the eyelids –

'... wake, my son!'

To the Saviour's voice and the B-flat diapason
57 octaves

below middle C emanating unheard
from a super massive black hole in the centre of the Perseus cluster –

is added Zarathustra-burgeon, rumble of organs,
contrabassoon and drum-clouds ...

three bloody strokes of dawn /

drawn on white grass ... Crusted, pink-rimmed eyes,
prints of worn trainers, trail of pram-wheels,

lead from the piss-house in the park, vanishing towards the main drag –

And back in the urinal,

among dead electric warriors of time –
ripped out verses from the bible scattered on the floor –

Daniel, Deuteronomy, Prophecies, Isaiah 43.15 –

I am the Lord, your Holy One, the Creator of Israel, your …

a blocked lavatory's gray breezeblock in red-dawn's
cracked-yellow-tiled Hospice of All Souls,

where, soiled newspaper floating among cack,

opens like some exotic African flower towards the light …

In Times Trashed ...

Among the poison-ivy, weapons of mass deception /
Bush dynasty connections with Carlucci and the Carlyle Group's
slam-dunk-billion $$$ Oil-Gold-War-on-Terrorism –

we find in times trashed of independent courts and the social contract,

the Harvard Business Review pushing reprints – viz.

How to Serve the Poor,
Profitably ...

And figuring among other shelved X files in which one child
starves to death every three seconds and two million workers die
from workplace events each year –

add these Globo-smash Incs. to your list:

British American Tobacco and Phillip Morris (still counting the body bags)
Johns Manville, the Cape Company, and Hardie Industries (lethal bastardy)
Nestle (infanticide) Ford, Dutch Shell, Occidental Petroleum,
Union Carbide, Exxon, Firestone (death with its many exits)

And for Enviro crimes / fraud /and or / corruption, theft, racism,

name – Bayer, Boeing, Citigroup, Coca-Cola, Credit Suisse, Daiwa Bank.
Hoffmann-Laroche, Royal Caribbean Cruises, TAP Pharmaceuticals,
Wal-Mart, Enron (the smartest guys in the room) etc.

... Even in our impuissant lives – where the government pursues
its 'geo strategies' by pissing on the heads of the unemployed,

dirty bowsers shoot through in winter rain spruiking
their 'new green clean energy' and a retailer in our local High St.,

runs this Lladro fine-china advert:

'Evocative, dreamlike, symbolism representing the longing
and desires of humankind, the flow of life, the quest
and discovery of reason, emotions and dreams …'

– as, in the same breath, I note a wall
by the Dead Animal Caff which, this morning, announced –

We aRE PeOPLe 2!

has been slobberdamned, sand-blasted off, by the tin-heads
screaming – this is our city, our planet, our universe ...

Now only a little oxide blood remains between the bricks

and carbon-monoxide ghosts wave the blue-collar traffic
home through darkening streets

where once the cornstalks waved …

Fire

Two men rush in:

'... we want your money!'

and stick the old man's hand in the fire.

A city block after dark. A moment
of dark-green-black adumbra: a cat on the roof

s.t.r.e.t.c.h.i.n.g...

incisors wide and gaping
in the star-struck night;

on the next level down –

a woman, illuminated
as from the beyond in a patch of light,
her face a Modigliani oval with almond eyes,

is watering two mandarin orange trees on her balcony:

she is also of the gasoline night, lights in her flesh,
the interface between two worlds
in which revelation and decline

become part of junk DNA
drifting down from not so-OK streets

and the insane dreams of U alone ... She hums under her breath,

watching ghosts flicker over the city through a sample of time
which curls back into itself, beautiful as hell-neon ...

On the next level down is the old man, his hand in the fire.

And on the ground floor,
in a garden of green-black shadow trees and shrubs
and a wall fronting the street –

a small dog, eyes axe-bright,
digs in to the pointing between the bricks,

shouting : 'Moon … moon!' …

caught over the city like the wind-child of ghosts between two skyscrapers.

There's an eye

There's an eye in the vortex of Alzheimer's
where blue flutters like Alice

and an old man with a stick fades out by the cemetery wall:

his arms,
his face

until the traffic calls, his skin heats like lead
or the sky claps its hands –

and stop!

STOP!

everything in
the clock …

the stone angels, the second hand, the gristle-bird – its beak open,
the poison hanging from the sky,

Transfixed,

one leg raised,
he stands there by the iron gates
among a pulse of blinding butterflies
slowly flexing their wings among a rush of sunspots,

waiting for one moment to tumble into another.

Then someone takes his hand:

his stick comes forward, his leg
followed by the next, then the stick again

as a child skips off, looking back over her shoulder:
'I like that grave – and that – and that ...'

A clear voice in the evergreen democracy of extinction.

In Gaudy Night

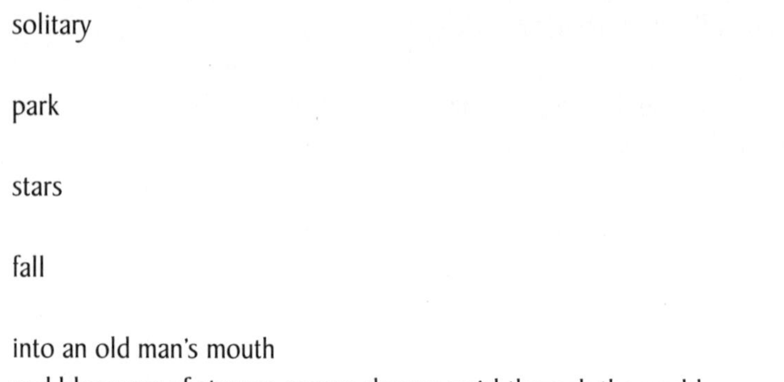

Time vaults above it
– while

solitary

park

stars

fall

into an old man's mouth
and blossoms of strange orange dreams swirl through the world.

But he is not alone – whichever way he turns on the night-wet grass,
an invisible wife turns with him:

knees up, a babushka, she fits like a wedding of ugly dolls,
bottom-to-crotch together under the bush –

at their feet, an in memoriam dog with huge eyelashes
and a killer-mouth

throbs in-out-in-out of existence

like a false dawn, tries to materialize, doesn't.
Occasionally, she raises her leg and her foot rubs his.

Attar of leaves rustle
a cop car howls round the zones of exclusion

while the dream goes on
rubbing a dirty finger inside his mouth

and moths of the night flutter around his shopping trolley,
his plastic bags,

which, of this world's goods, all-in-all, might amount

to about of $^{2}/_{3}$ of $^{1}/_{5}$ of fuck-all…

Not to be wondered, then, he groans and moans,
among strange orange dreams,

when half the day is gaudy night in the sacred forest –

and it's all his …

The True Light

High over the swarm-cells of the world,

swaying skyscrapers,
mass extinctions –

a graph line after dark extends from earth-core
to a point in blank infinity… the polished

axis of facilitators and bagmen.

The Hang Seng, bubbling furiously,
the Dow Jones, brilliant strobes

killing the stars over New York,
Paris-London-Berlin *noir.*

True Light of True Light –

the Crack-Ecstasy fever-dream of the money-laundering
Afghan-Chechen-Viet

Colombian drug trade grossing

twelve hundred billion dollars per –

And still firing, where it's hot to trot tonight,
The Docks, outside the Dead Animal caff,

with low voices by the coffee machine,

(down Calcutta St., black echo-footstep-shuffle of the dead
marking their boundaries)

– Someone coughs in the shadows, a lighter flares,

and a whore points
to the warehouse roof a jumper went off last night,

tracing the graph line up through moon-drift,
poison vapour over the city –

past lost worlds

to where the rest of the Universe is either burning or rusting …

Terse

Such is the floral entrance to our Estate

(where the council last year planted
a job lot of roses in building spoil)

and Mrs O'Connor, poor old cow, traipsing back
to the tower block with her shopping – being suddenly

overtaken by a fit of coughing …

looks to choke among sudden forcefields of concrete,

but gets the better of it, rolls the wad with dust
round her mouth,

spits it into her hand for inspection

before tossing the phlegm with a meaty flick
into the bushes

where it hangs green and sloppy
from the twigs of a dying Madame President …

A statement, which, in this Age of the Terse and Centrelink,

might be about as good as it gets –

wouldn't you say?

Art

Through clay-seep, by dawn's first light,
the railway cutting –

among coloured chemical pools and factory demolitions,

I'm waiting for first thrum! morning Intercity Express, fast, intensive,

past the Signal Box – And how pleasurably cool-wild elderberry,
and silver rails among blackberry drip through the mist.

Spider-worlds, festooned, minute and spun-wisp,
hang from unopened flower to flower.

And in the distance, beyond the hills,

more old webs where tiny cripples and bankrupts hang
from silky ropes among lost stars over Venture City …

hearts ripped out like dry bacteria,
their corpses twist this way and that in the sky,

while the abyss soars above itself –

Early morning, the first tip of the sun

    vanishing into pale-blue-green –

    stone canyons,

yr. actual nasty life imitating art …

The Searchers

With bursts of pheromones

in this night is young – thousands
searching for the Lode – the Key
to the Treasure Game.

Crowds and loners, dreaming.

Like robots going round and round
under Venture City's flashing neon
and topless bars, strange creatures,
derelicts,
shit kickers
of the night,
Dead St. processions.

To taste the ambience of the quest, stand here among the lights.
Lose self in the gape and uvula of possibilities

slowly winding and unwinding its helix and shining electrodes
among the stars:

poison dwarfs and cop cars,
wanderers and cripples with wild surmise
the faces of bankrupts, soo brill-i-antly outshone moon
and long stretch limos in a planet of ravening shadows

Where logos flash like gambling machines
and all the girls are moaning

for the sailor
home from the Seven Sleaze and the Milky Way

on leave to this Utopia beyond that distant shore …

You hear it said in the wilderness of joy where dog-eats-dog-eats-shit

in that phantom voice to which all dreams converge
in a scream of white light from a distant star

I want the world.
I want it now …

Like you're one of the damned and forever lost
waking naked in a weird and filthy place,
a strange new sun rising from your mouth…

Tired

Sweet ambience
of tiny-breasted of attendants
leaking Sacred Damema Milk:

as one takes my
shoes, another brings Dilmah tea in a cup

with a peacock neck.

So cooled by punkah-wallah fans,
legs crossed, eyes closed,
in the shade

of an plastic orange Taj Mahal,

I listen to wistful sighs the transmigration of souls make
in tall coconut trees in Cheap-as-Chips

tossing fateful signs of the Zodiac
from aisle to aisle:

the splash and surf of Hawaii,

the balalaika sounds of Aladdin Cotton underpants
intermingled with the love-moan of Tai plastics, Burmese carvings
Chinese braces …

the scream of joss-sticks
ear-rings, glass parrots, green walruses … monkeys, bamboo charms.

While, the feel of the store – the tilt of it slides from side-to-side
under a jeweled howdah – Down past foundations
into the fastness of the planet,

into meat and muscle — the roll of Buddha-bones

as the Great Gray Cosmic elephant moves trumpeting through the Galaxy –

Free Trade, Global Warming, the Melting Arctic,
rocking backwards and forwards…

carrying us all through time, our town, Chinese chimneys,

Jeb's Secondhand, Cash 'n Treasure
– Cap'n Kidd's and the Main Rd.

like a Glittering Trashcan on its Head …

The String

Sounds the echo of an old hymn through a stone Narthex
and big double doors,

'... *There's a Fountain Of blood*
    drawn from Emmanuel's veins...' Past the church

and the old woman humming it,
the first testicles of the stars hanging from the sky

over the Retirement Village as she rounds the corner into High St.,

into ... Action-Men, lights, traffic, –
Giant Blow-Up Santa Clauses leap from carpark to carpark.
store detectives, plastic bags,

and the whole weak/massive energy of Xmas arches in a parabola
over the suburb ...

One leg then another, very slowly, past the Uniting Church,
a string on her wrist tied to her little dog,
Mrs Mouldybrokes slithers her Zimmer frame.

Up the High St., past chops and blood-sausage bags
hanging from Woolworths 'at today's best prices' ...

Under the flashing kosher/ goyescher lights,
and all the happy families...

Very tall and thin, Mr Striding Legs,
clouds in his hat, waves them on
past the traffic lights:

'This way, Mrs Mouldybrokes. This way!'

The dog snuffles in market cabbage leaves,
pisses on a likely post –

but drawn on by the Technology of hell and the leash, shuffles, farting.

Past dead chickens odours and abattoirs,
feathers, dead carpets –

and Mrs Mouldybrokes humming the tune:

'Dear dying Lamb, Thy precious blood shall never lose its power …'

And later –

'Redeeming love has been my theme …'

under the Overpass where people lean over, waving:

'… Mrs Mouldybrokes! Happy Xmas, Mrs Mouldybrokes …'

step-by-step – and it's where she is going now with her dog – up the High St.,
past the Cement Works and the New Houses towards

the King's Palace and the hills beyond

with her Walker.

Those statues on the sidewalk in white –

Waverers who looked back and were struck to instant salt.

Church-leaves

Is it residual power from the Sunday baptisms –

or a last gleam that fades into
the dirty flowers of the city upside down in the head
of the Concrete Steeple-Christ ...?

A spatter of rain,

the wind gusting like raw flesh,

blows Leaf Men with sharp stick teeth down the street:
winter colours whirling with rubbish among cars and pedestrians
affirming ass-to-gas, time-to-slime,

by tossing cracked bells
and vestry clocks in the air –

or piss
in gutter frouche-cups where very thin tall shadows
of pedophile-priests in silver masks,

lost in graves and trees, wind-hiss of Redemption by the church,

rear up like shafts and vanish through contemplation
and the overcast as if still fusing with the infinite ...

cars beep!

traffic lights
in murk
flash

Eucharist,
Eucharist
Eucharist

Tithes

Tithes and rents!
Tithes and rents!
Tithes and rents!

a belled-boom

pull on Evensong ropes,

hell's double-toll!

big bells' bell,
cobbled lanes,
medieval psych waves.

A millennium of pure Gamma rays
menace, squalor, hanging, putrefactions,
and death …

a missal of saints' bones, glanders, and murder –
seeped into stone and iron:

all pinnacles, spires, and castellation,

fold upon fold soars upwards – The Bleeding Saviour,
a dead Che Guevara, caught in the electric field

of tortured Jerusalem, mad popes,
and the black lightning strokes of *heil und gothic* …

a string of raw rosary beads,

draped over a blood cross reared against the virtual sky of an alien planet
and ragged clouds,

where pure, high and clean tonight,

a Hacker's Moon floats
over the South Transept,

in the new banditry …

News Flash

From the Dead Sea Scrolls,

a trickle of words blackens into a pool. A blood headline,
among the Passover of bad-breath ghosts

and crimson-staining, falls through the sky.

All it needs is a little more cachexy and cacodemon,

another tattered foreskin blowing down the street,
or a stream of menses –
squeeze on the tampon,

terror howl from the Munch-mask – And you –

all it needs is you, feet up,
a plate of choccy biscuits on your knee,

time-traveller among the screams and
dust of a flyblown day drifting up some filthy TV street.

Stories with no moral, illegal as terror-war, futile, tatty-nasty, body parts …

Flash! Flash! of children, bellies, bleeding vulvas.

We love you! 9.11, Gaza, Lebanon, Baghdad
crawling round your womb like a cockroach:
splash of blood on the windscreen. Fire! Smoke!

Rockets, Humvees. And deathdeathdeath.
Sweet Somethinging Death, where are you wandering

with all yr. re-runs, bells ringing, end of year good wishes.

(Pass me another tissue, scream-face!

Can't help masturbating again)

Last stop

First, a last pitstop,
an emptying of body fluids

before you return with history in a Greyhound bus
and the old iron gates of the morning swing open to the city

where ancient blood-polyps
of the past have lived before.

Same garbage cans.
Same fast-food spattered car yards of phlegm and angst
The Green Man pub still traveling through space with boarded windows
The black Job-Search-Factory on the hill

And the fish-line tangled, river-lapping barges and slums
in continued silver-fuse with the infinite

overlaid by scaggy brown and first snakes of sunrise
hissing on crumbling windowsills in silent

return to streets and public urinals – Outer Mission St.,
the Sisters of Charity – old parole territory

and dawn's last stop for the Greyhound's sss! of opening doors.
Passengers, grabbing holdalls,
vanish

into the hum of solenoids and low-grade waste – an eternity of gamma rays
beamed up from old Fish Wharves and the black slush ingested
by compacters that circle forever
between the poles,

but low and traveling faster over the cliffs of time
than you have ever seen before …

Suddenly, a buzz on the cell phone:

a quick message from hell –
the warm voice of yr. slum landlord welcoming his tenants home …

Slow

Cake. More cake –
you hear it said by pensioners.

It's the pull of atoms,
the weight of earth

– a whisper.
– a shrug behind their back

Poor dears, eyes like watery paper, slow as sticks,

vague as slopping tea
in a caff among sunheaps of traffic fumes

by the dim, all-seeing wastes of the Universe:

(Excuse me, grandma: may I see you across the road?)

It's their bodies

(with all the ghosts blowing past,
why should death take so long …?)

Cisterns flushing, tap-tap of a stick at night
in the kitchen,

a rib-cage glimmer through crêpe-y flesh:

tea ,.. let's make some tea,
two sugars … cake! A slice of Bi-Lo. A sandwich. Some fruit loaf …

And butter. More butter … *it's good for you!*

Like masks of auto-destruct.

Crumbling jaws.

Skulls riving their way through the planet
while children starve …

City Sunset Fahrenheit

In a CBD flash of the divine – '*last minute contract with life –*'

street-ghosts and futures traders elbowing past,
fall off into gold-sky-molten-vat-heaven

because only God has so much money …

This hour of City Sunset Fahrenheit.

Strong rooms, yellow graves
streets on fire, the dancing dead with daffodil eyes –

won't you take my hand, madam …

Like a cruel money-wind sweeping the planet

– all your moaning fantasies
in one gigantic billionaire jewel-box.

The Cullinan diamond,
Fort Knox,
the 50, 000 Dow Jones:

Everyone outnumbered by slow burn of escalators and skyscrapers

(O love me forever
you greedy-seedy five-o'clock shadow planet!)

Until a child points …

over the Empire mansions

to where time, brassily flocculating over the city,
shrivels into edges drawn into puckers.

And a faraway flute is heard playing in the shadow of the Stock X –

So wild and high,
with such sweet sorrow.

The day is ending –
and there is nowhere left to hide.

Like 3-4-Parent Satyrs …

Like the wail of a glass spirit
caught by 3-4-Parent Satyrs –

slither of rubber gloves – or a G.M. egg, triumphant stem-cell,
and a see-thru womb writhing and gasping

in test-tube night:

'I didn't!'
'You did…'

and not a moment too soon

as more wild lies
plunge through the centrifuge

and everyone starts taking off their clothes again.

Suddenly, a light flashes,

a wriggling foetus,
a rudimentary eye opening in a black-glass mirror.

Who am I …
What's happening …?

Like a megabucks-ray probing the fontanel –

the Big Gizmo, screech of atoms,
earth opening its money-rat-trap
of freeways,
bowels, ovaries,
lust

for the whatjemecallit – the Second Coming:

our vision of light cloned and fleering off
through strange flickerings of time

and ancient babycrap …

Behold! says the angel in the wet-dream with his Weenie-knife

(bloodstained wings, holding up the kid's blessed foreskin
from which the future's born)

I bring you more tidings of great woe …

Sprites

A gash /stroke-mouth   a slow-dark
of shadows,

then a fluid dimorphic bulk, suddenly engrailed,

flares in-and-out of this night-world's bashed-in cheekbones.

A petrol-flicker of lightning over his left shoulder –
among the caffs and shuttered Mall shops,
he scrounges from sand-barrels –
camels-escorts-winfields-cools-virginia slims-morris –
horizon-silver-tips,

maybe getting lucky with tossed reefers: unknown shit,
a coin or t-three …

He lurches past McBastard's and Cheap-as-Chips
dragging a varicose leg, vanishes again back-end of restaurants and bins –

until thunder-roll -storm-break!

and his face washes back down the Mall, neck-clay
imprinted with mesh –

one of Picasso's impoverished children,

a triangle of lightning,

an arm projecting from the amorphous,
and a reinterpreted shape in night of tall visions

among dark permanganate-red of the unknown / threats /

shouting mirrors / in which all money is hell.

Same dollar ticket

Same dollar ticket will get *you* there:

a blare an aerosol of dead cells,
an old man coughing lung-garbage
front seat
of the hospital bus: as one paroxysm
follows another

– they drift like black holes,
up the aisle …

Two poor old slags, a single pregnant.

A butterfly,
with a wing-ectomy, flutters beyond reach,
an old woman with a basket, another with stained
cotton wool in her ears, a pair of crutches,
a pale girl with a shaved head …

a jig-saw puzzle for a cripple,
a bunch of grapes –

while Spring, on giant scaly legs keeps pace,
banging on the windows with sprays
of cherry blossom and narcissi:
a stained concrete mask, singing like a phoenix,

and flashing pixels! pixels!

with Deadsville images whirling past – back streets,
arms, legs, sick mouths,
a bell-jar of worms …

while the bus trundles on,

past pubs, a junkyard,
and the gray cliffs of Housing Commission tower-block
with dried noises hanging from the sky –

to our first stop – by the public X-ray Dept.
and the scuffed swing-doors –

hunched figures hesitating by the entrance to a run-down Underworld

where the dead are transfigured into light,
bone-by-bone …

Three Flags

If
you
haven't

a match –

piss
on
it

(he said)

– testimony of a lone bystander caught
in accretion of world fury

while time
points

a gun

among the stars…

* *

Bravely
the
flag
flaps

from
the
townhall
mast

a
flash
of
white

where the suburbs
string out behind

and rain collects in the bank accounts of ghosts …

*   *

Like
    Coke
        obesity

and fries

for the disenfranchised –

a ragged T shirt emblazoned

    'AVE A GOODWEEKEND'

Oz-emblem
over
the
left
tit

shares space
with the moon

on a shithouse floor …

where tall pharaohs
in golden masks

are urinating in the stalls.

You can hear them remote and ghostly,
whispering in the dark,
                                                  waiting for tomorrow

            which will be otherwise,

while the wind goes on counting its fingers in an empty condom dispenser

I an' I
I an' 2

in the random idiocy of time.

Origami

… for a feast of body bags

– crease the map
over Oil wells
and un-negotiated trade agreements.

Or for an Origami paper-boat,
a kneeling Arab
lit by divine light, and a river of shit flowing round the world – fold

Washington through Baghdad, Ohio through Mosul,
General Motors through Saudi Arabia.

In eighteen easy paper-moves – you can have the Peace Crane
fishing for maggots in the same river as Lebanon –

or the *hadith* in the beard of the Prophet flying round the world,
high over the desert and the bombed Palaces of Redemption,
arms out in blessing

singing *ognea …ga ognea…moagaha ga ognea* *
to the black, hundred thousands of blah-filled skins

of the *mustad'afun fi'l-ard, folded hands, sheet-wrapped-faces of the dead*
blowing round the desert in the certainty of happiness

while being played to by the giant depleted uranium flutes of time …

* nursery rhyme singing of young children

The Stone Ladder

Blame whatever – the gene-defects of the poor,
their slummy breast-milk
or the screams of their greasy brats

which hang over an urban nightmare like the light of a dirty Sanctus.

– Or trace their history back to the city and its tenements,
the sweat-shop enterprises,
the teller machines,

the gorges,
the rivers of decaying streets,

past where life strives and tries …

to the Costa del Crime, the alleys,
the potholes and demolitions

until the way stops by the Salvo's Outlet dead of night

– our concrete-block-and-galvo nod
to the socially stuffed. Our stained mattresses, our myriads of pictures,
Munch Screams, Woolworth prints, worn bras, pants, dresses,

human used-by-dates, deaths, all in packed skips, racks, aisle upon aisle –

tainted by the warmly sickening ineradicable smell of bums 'n tits,
under-arms, menses and middle class shit that smells of violets …

Epoch of wire hangers, rags and whiffs of violence:

and back of the store,

a rickety stone ladder propped up through the skylight
against a sacred picture of the moon,

rising above streets, clouds and night haze –

in which you can just make out the hole through which time is vanishing…

Boeing-Boeing

A beggar in Mumbai,
a Vietnamese girl planting rice in old killing fields,
a man leading a buffalo,

look up –

at the White House, the World Bank and Abu Ghraib
rising through the air on a wing.

– 4 ENGINES: PRATT & WHITNEY 22,680 kg THRUST (EACH)
JT9D TURBOFANS

59. 64 m span
70. 51 m length
19.33 m height

clawing, jets tearing
open

the invisible

peeling it back –

over third-world-dumping grounds,
a tin-opener in the void

roaring like a Battleship Galactic and Guantanamo Bay together.

Dazzled, a building worker

outside Patel's Sari Mart. ... looks up!

One of the child-labourers in a dawn Pakistan slate quarry smashes his hand
and a Knuckle Booms El / Diesel 10 / 17m operator in Karachi
                                        puts on dark glasses –

as colour implodes into mirage – razor wire,
– attack dogs on the leash of euros, pounds, dollar notes …

millions upon millions, blood-rainbows of the eternal
over the poverty cliffs of time,

an unreachable translucence drifting down
which suffuses the sky like the sores and stained rags of forbidden love,

while gradually fading to a speck, a mote, then nothing
on the superhighways of life –

but still can not vanish …

Ah! Vesperal!

The great Masturbators of Time …
scudding-cloud-puddles
outlaw galaxies
all your fantasies –

all the trillions of dark, skulking, hidden planets …

ululancy

bipedality

brutal XXX files with their payload of death

and poxy neuters in orb and sorrow
at the fall of man …

Like fateful spirogyra,

crotches, hair, eyes of stone, the scream of plastic bags
emerging from the mud:

'Hey! dig those stars …'

Our local toy town.

400 billion galaxies glittering down.

Our wildest dreams laced with poison robots,
and private enterprise poly-programmed in, gripping the same soil

as all the terror zones
and mirror flashes in your average urban nightmare.

All that real estate up there …

Our Terra Nullius among the carrion hordes

The wailing of Giant Flutes in the Black Magellanic Clouds
The Nebulosity in Cygnus …

Like star-wanderers through our days:

Like the warm taste of earth-sperm
back of the throat

we call 'going home …'

A Maugre

A maugre on the energy of this Milky Wheel,

thunder of girders, drop-forge hammers,

and screams of female crotch-hairs
fluttering in the wind.

Shrill perfumed shouts of '*More! more!*'

more warehouses, roads, exurbs hiving off like amoebae,
power station, beggars, street-kids ...

while the sky buckles under the weight of the cocked-up legs of insatiable instinct

and the glitter-dreams of dumpsters among broken glass
and sacred birthstones whose mystic power

overflows with grotesquerie, nutmeggy-smells and huge Raphaelesque
dimpled wrists. They jut from their membranes, giants' feet,

stained mattresses , fatty womb-waters, rivers of bones, while
famished estrogens and vagina musk blow round the planet.

They say of those crap pipes in the city that tilt our effluent out
beyond the stars –

put your ear to one of these
and you'll hear the scream and suck of all the pregnancies in the world

come to term...

Nocturne

Call them vagrant noctilucents,
glimmers here-and-there,
vanishing – reappearing,

tiny gas spurts in the dark ,

minute eyelids, touched,
fluttering with exhausted light

of husks underground being drawn out
with incredible osmotic strength

v.e.r.y. t.h i.n   v e.r.y l.o.n.g.

Molecules of bones and flesh-fruits in long coloured ribbons,
waving and undulating

through soil, crystal lattices, curling round
minute stones and first fine root-tendril-tip

of cemetery trees – which tower up through transfigured night –

into skeins of ghost-mirrors
and frost-glitter …

In the grass below, a few methane sparklers between each grave

to light the purple skin-bridge between the stars.

Night in Vortex

Night in vortex, those dreams
and what images, what buildings
rising and falling like the sea

while the sleepers drift in their K-mart pajamas.

High over suburbs
and the wind-terraces of the dark,

weightless as leitmotivs sucked up into nude-swirl
and megaforce,

they leave Elysium-effluvium behind, a plunging funnel of black fog,
a world creating and recreating itself among miles of twisted piping,
a giant arm that waves among the wreckage and vanishes,

and gas belches through the clouds as hapless souls of stone streets
and railways are flung out with cries of wild iron

from this poisonous centrifuge
into the zig-zag of lightning and computers which forever circle the globe

and real money never sleeps …

O Mother of all men.

Megapolis! Cruel combo of whatever the guttural cock
and sweating uterus can dream – perversions, animadversions
coupling of teller machines, skyscrapers

– a giant skull with infected eyes that rolls to the end of the world

and listens to the cries of all time
like butterflies with broken legs among the stars

their voices picked clean as a whistle …

The Pipe

Time that blows its early morning lovelessness,
a tatty-ragged
wind

flapping a torn black / white poster on a wall
with awesome powers of emptiness.

Waterloo Rd., Bessemer St ...

Bedsitterland,

Past closed TAB, acid greens, poxy neuters
to where site-flags wave over plastic Porta-Barriers

enclosing an excavation:
a Telecom manhole-cover,

old gas / water mains.

A trench, a layer
of clay-sands mixed with bricks and old tarmac

overlying stained pedal-clays with Council infill

from the Cretaceous – in turn, reveal a sewage-pipe
laid on Devonian sandstone

which was once a hundred-foot-high red/ scarlet-banded bluff

at whose base a misty river flowed

towards some distant sea
when reptiles ruled the world ...

The Window

After the thunder – sudden rain-emptying clouds
scattering the toxic spirits of the night,

gutters run a city's filthy mouthwash

(dead-bowel rubbish, ghosts and confetti
swept along)

the storm moves away:

– a scud moon flashes like giant
white squid bottom of ten thousand grids …

Suddenly, a barred window in the sky opens:
a hard-assed vice-cop in a blood-flecked shirt

leans out; his eyes rove suspiciously over tiny
lamp-lit streets staring up through K and Crack

of treacherous time into the Inkyvoid
and the coolly raging firewalls of the Universe

Headlights sweep the sky: neon flickers in the CBD.

Nearby, the town-hall clock starts to toll the hour.

3 o'clock!

And all's well.

Yeahyeahyeah

Up before the Youth Court,
Sir Gawain Wanker the Millionth
and his chinless bro.

filthy escutcheon with knuckles rampant,

are accompanied by single, raddled, goitrously grinning parent
yeahyeah ...

wellwewuzlikeshitfaced
fuck-to-do

likeanwewuzjustlike

clay on their trainers,
in their loveless locks

an axe-and-crowbar moonlit trail (as charged)
of hacked, whacked, gouged, and otherwise booted-in
classic heads, legs, private parts etc.

of our local cemetery...

O REST IN THE LORD. WAIT PATIENTLY FOR HIM

with one Gavin X's monument among the holocaust,
age 5, sorely missed by middle class yuppie parents
and female sibling (BACCALAUREATE GRAD.)

a broken column
and a cherub in the grass

still pointing upwards to where Playschool vanished ...

Quite a crowd

Where there was nothing,
now quite a crowd of us.

First a wind,
then papers swirl cleansing the streets of filthy dreams –

and an old man on a bench with his plastic bags
who watches the High Wooden Horses of Night
staring over traffic lights

at a fountain flashing diamante

wavering and swaying,

as it dances naked in the cobbled Mall.

Suddenly, a star clicks a reel of film in its camera,

a tiny spark
between two scudding clouds.

Then it vanishes, still taking pictures.

'Remember us to the rest of the Universe …'

I will …

Counterpoint

Fly-songs and the nacreous spoon of morning sun
stirs them behind The Caff like buzzing electrodes
in a blackened plug …

'sszzeezh phezee eee saazz
phzz zz !'

– Sounds heard by Dwarf Woman, who exudes strangeness,
– a haze of blackheads, sitting on
the pavement, feet in the gutter, beside
a small street-flower, leaves bent over
by the fatal weight
of the morning sun.
She joins in the fly-chorus – thin-screams … a fifth above:

'Tra-la-la
            Traalaalalaa!'

And the dying plant replies with counter subject –

Mmmmmmm   mmmmmmmmm m m   m   m   m

So an excerpt from the score reads:

Zz pzz mm   mm
            tra   la   m
la m ssz   zzz
                  la   mmmm   pfss   mm
tra   la   phzz
                  zzz sz zss
            phzz   tra
                        mmm   wei

mmm   m   la

A hymn of blood sacrifice to early traffic on its way,
and eighteen-wheel semis air-braking at red lights:

– a wind from far-off reed plains in the brickwork
winding and weaving among the counterpoint – a wild flute singing
'… la-de-da-dee-da-dee-doh …'

for these, crowned with hyssop, the morning with tulip clouds,
and all creeping, shining creatures

of infected time …

Nevermind

Nevermind the screams,

foul entropy
roar of the synchronous

– all the orifice-seepings,
dirt, hairs, body noises, squeal of plastic bags:

the streets go round and round and round

our lives go round

and all we need is Mmmm!

(turn back the sheets
and count the mattress stains)

all we need is Lerve!

all we need,
all we

all

al

a

Post Mortem

As the scalpel slides from throat to crotch,
the right claw still grips the flag.
Through burnt-crisp,
half-cooked fat,

the heart

slips down to join the liver beside a blood-lake
where post 9.11 tank-tracks in the sludge
run out of sight beyond
Ramalla,

the Vena Cava, the spleen and curve of ribs,

to the place in which the womb-blastocyst, embedded in its endometrium,
first folded inwards on itself
to become

the intimation of a spinal cord

12 years ago …

Spring

Spring as it happens at night – a sudden hubbub in Dock St.,
No time to waste, a hurry of excited pubes,
testes and ovaries

waving sex and flowers

rush pell-mell through Sleep-City,
a blossoming of white cement-dust
mingling with mignonette of pheromones

signals yet another year of bastardry and dalliance

with Shakespeare-Marlowe-Jonson's
Spring-a-Ding on the wasteland by the pub coming in …

Likewise the biggest rodents
scuttling under the floorboards of the town,
the best cockroach bait,

and the dirtiest rentals as they froth or bud
among fractals and relentless Fibonacci forces
squatting behind closed factories and forever.

You can breathe their sacred love-names in the dark,

The Love Tree by the urinal

Love spread-eagled on the dole,
Love with the rags up. Love-lies-bleeding.
Love-in-idleness.
Love with its face rearranged by a Centrelink ball-peen hammer …

Look where each plant and sweet branch-crackle
– with multilateral leaf-frets, friezes,
climbers, blossoms and finials, are reflected

in sudden star-warehouse-window-flash –

And where, for a brief moment in the Milky Way,
every building flutters a dirty handkerchief …

Wandering Road

You'll know it when the bus arrives through the endless plains,

a passing cloud burning off in the sun –

but shaped vaguely like a wandering,
mongrel soul

in slow drift over a drunken, child incest,
        black-white-wife-beating country town …

dispersing, into wax-melt, metal roof-eye / brutal rays

and virulent head-swim – soft-mouthed brink of the blue abyss …

O Settler graves.

Dirty Pub, Cardboard Cutout
of the outback and the Tourist Board

Kingdom of woeful shit and starving sheep.

Someday a wind or fire will come to this place
its bones hissing like poison,
and scour it to the dust.

It will become nothing but air.

A wandering road of pink pollen and violet crocuses in the sky …

Territory

Between high razor-wire fence, Patel's Grocery Warehouse,

and the railway line, a last territorial prayer
for the dying day

– our hard-case blackbird on a high pole sings

fuck youoouu
fuck youuuoo
fuck youyouooo …

Over the wasteland other roughnecks respond,
Dock St. to Walter-to-Edinburgh,

from waterfront to suburb,
suburb-to-suburb –

suburb to country

fuck youoo!
fuck youyyyoo …

and ever further
and further

more dimly, distantly among church spires
and villages

echoes:

f.u... k y. o.u. c.k. y..u

f.u. y…

(a rustle of nesting leaves from the topmost bough of a tree
where a darkening hollow, white with birdshit,

is lit by the solitary eco-lux of an evening star)

The Invitation

Birds waste no time

when dawn

like an Aztec chook
beats at the window …

– Flash of gold
and streaming
moon X-rays,

this miraculous Rooster in a strutting ruby

– from which Alighieri himself peers between bars of shit
and a flicker of blinding tumescent nerves,

blares through glass, past
highrise still wet with sperm and sex,

A gaudy gaudete, tobacco-cough-blast of infra red
and graveland juicing phlegm

hitting the pavements with swirls of the unbelievable –

while embracing you / this now / at the heart of it,
– the zombie palette-heart of the ballsy bird,

whose splash-ectoplasm, part mildew-eating death,

and million dirty colours scatter these wrecked beds
and cloud-hordes of doubloons over the city –

in flash / flash / flash! of bloody feathers.

Vanishing ...

in the rhetoric of transience and snot,

back to the Temple of Light –

soft zoom-up over moaning traffic lights
and hills afire –

Return to the Blue-Eyed Kingdom

– early-morning-scream-skies of the Universe ...

Dirty Eyes

Cries from the zoo
like strips of dry flesh dangling from the moon
or the scream of a toucan in broken glass –

their last rotten dream
bellows
dirty eyes,
rattle of bars

as
all wake:

the OOO AHHHH
ascending/descending,

castrati screaming the Five Sorrowful Mysteries,
their morning prayer
muzzles smeared with bacteria pointing skyward,

sounds rising up as from the furthest shores
of beginning mixed with points grinding,
faraway railcar shunting,

high over the city

then spreading out over the suburbs, strip malls,
concrete lawns, and the inexorable world of '*how it is*'

higher and higher

an opus of smoke vanishing between the stars

while the galaxies slowly decant their turds
from one chamberpot to another

and darkness slowly cuts itself another asshole
for dawn to peer through

Wings

Beautiful as a print of a Painted Lady exiting the machine,
a late Autumn butterfly alights
on my sleeve …

and a child points, stepping closer to the pulse and throb

of four moons,
and the solenoids

connecting the anti-rust of stars
and the direction of the current flowing through its wings:

A moment's
hiatus for admiration

then away! it flits down the shopping Mall

to Paris, Strasbourg or wherever they're giving away sunsets,

each flap of its wings
closing a door behind in space –

a green-on-rim-fire,
steel-blue, a yellow-purple,

higher and higher among the concrete flowers
and metal stalks of the city

where arrogant mirrors flash their megawatts,

and Street Ghosts wave

goodbye
goodbye.

It will be torn to pieces by a savage world.

It will live forever …

Wisp

A sometime-teacher's sad slow drift over the city, legs, arms straight out,
blue butterflies fluttering on her eyelids,

a light wavering through
a city's poxy biosphere and passing high over Woolworths …

before gradually morphing to suburb-sunset-wisp,

a pink silk scarf being stroked and twisted
into rare moments of embossed light, a sun-gift
of Chinese-crimson, dragon-gold …

Until, like invisible beings (in gouache of the sacred –

coloured molecules drifting in reality dysfunction –
from Church-to-Council crematorium
towards sunset)

her remains waver slowly over high-rise buildings, creeping home
to the streets and car-yards of the labyrinth –

before gradually dispersing in deconstructed gauze,
inside of light-within-light of a life –

filmy drape, slow sift,

among layer-upon-layer of air, high pylons
and all the anon. of the Matrix …

– where brick veneer-flash-fibro-car windscreens,

morse code/ flare like a signal …

Iron Butterflies

... these Westering clouds!

just the moment for iron-butterflies
        and black anvil-scarlet-clouds to splurge

in last picture-show: sky-scraper
windows semaphoring

Texas Crude! Sweat Shops of Asia Inc!

calling Head Office – calling Head Office ...

A sacred sunset of commercial haze
over the rail-yards,

a purpling violet with penumbra-adumbra

seeping through – past the Cement Works,
the old Water Towers, the factories –

darkening suburb roofs, chimneys – and touching
the Council's forgotten demolition dump of bricks and plaster

on a wasteland verge where evening grows among the weeds.

Suddenly a flight of loft-pigeons breaks into last
wing-glint-red-rush:

first bat-radar-swoops

round a blooper-star, a radio in an old car
bursts into side-street-life. Then voices

from a backyard

and these images of time in a darkening world.

Three wickets chalked on a urinal wall by the pub.
and a steel-drum at the bowler's end ...

What's immortal?

This is immortal...

Monet's Boat

... Sadly, there's a storm of money in this picture –
cash in suitcases and paper bags ...
the readies, a whirlwind of Monet-Monopoly

pouring from all the clouds, sewers, and orifices of the world,

(numbered Swiss accounts, bearer bonds)

Where the sun, shadowing cruel cliffs is a violin
tied with red ribbons ...

– to the horizon, a mass of
diamonds, rubies, sapphire-paint

sea-ripple-shimmering shhh! shh! – around and far out –

and the land-bound, iris-leaf-bearded-mummified Monet,
straw hat and cane, slumps

in a rowing-boat ...

Suddenly, a puff of wind through the silk-cocaine-and wildflower sky

off Cap d' Antibes flashes its radar
water flashes back

like a giant mirror: Prism! Prism!

The swell-rocks but the corpse and the boat are motionless

Then a gull sweeps past, a rose tattooed on its forehead,
and the colour-mirage drifts ashore, foamfall whisper –
a vagrant dazzle-dazzle, lifts it again
into salt Rainbow! Rainbow!

Up! Up!

until, everything is sparkfire red / blue/ shading phosphorescence –
intimate as an inside-red-miracle-sex-mouth among waving fronds
where the boat is suspended

in a forest of waving weeds, sea-anemones, sand
and all the flashing star creatures
in the pleasure grounds of tide …

The Weighing

Like voyages through old maps,
time seems to have no accounting
among these green-blue spirits of the deep.

Stone lions on eternal plinths roar intermittently at the sea
curving round into mirror-infinity.

Smooth black cliffs
tower over an island channel.

And an enigmatic Mediterranean, in mask and white gloves,
lays a line of stained tongues sprinkled with sesame
by the fishermen's cottages.

An afternoon of sleeping taverns
and a faraway blue trawler sailing through its own reflection,

where, on a stone wharf,
a white shark,
a long red flower in its mouth,

is being weighed and foto-flashed.

Two men, with the air of those who have returned from a voyage round the world
or some vast enterprise involving the moon,

stand ankle-deep among fish-blood and guts,
their arms raised in victory.

Sun glitters on chunky male jewelry and the universal brotherhood of man …

while mysterious energy swirls and vanishes about their million-dollar-boat
– the god-force still strong upon it –

with its killing platform, straps and chair,
as it slowly sails up a dazzling ascension of champagne waterfalls in pure light
between two beds of ice …

becoming more distant, then smaller – smaller

– shrinking into a tiny blood-stained sunburst
you might wear in a pendant forever.

Picture

Height and light crowned by a domed roof

captures a singularity of space
with elegance…

Where echoing footsteps
on tessera

ascend marble stairs, pass along corridors
through mirrors into more mirrors

of the Art Gallery
and everything is revenant or dead.

Dead paint; dead frames, dead names

while the real business of the world goes on outside.

People fuck sheep
and eat spiders:

faces zoom in and out of focus,

all under a sky of iron gall, tannins and iron sulphates
in which the Book of Revelation is written.

Where children cry, madmen chase the sunrise
and people stop to watch two poor old dossers,

boots tied with string, struggling with a picture from the Park:

whose colours are a megaburst, a palette of hot metal-dust
and a terrible fluttering of wings – from which Autumn Lady
leans down from a Sun-frame

to comfort the dead as they swim up through the earth,
appear, then vanish behind bars of grass.

But when she transcends as leaves, real leaves from trees,
by rippling round the curvature of the world,
to emerge brilliantly, arms wide
                                        like a whore from a brothel,

you only need one painting.